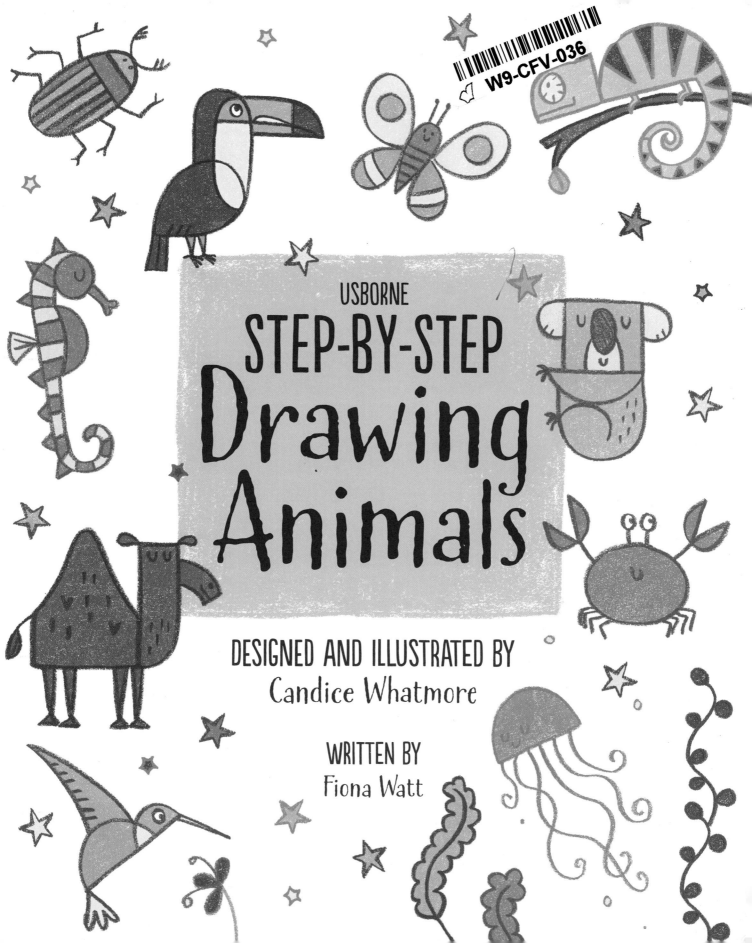

USBORNE
# STEP-BY-STEP
# Drawing
# Animals

DESIGNED AND ILLUSTRATED BY
Candice Whatmore

WRITTEN BY
Fiona Watt

# How to draw a fox

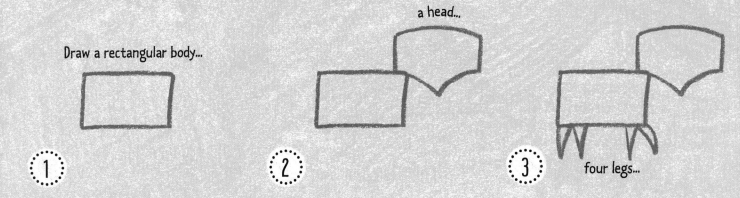

Draw a rectangular body...

a head...

four legs...

① ② ③

Your turn...

a bushy tail...

two pointed ears...

a line on the chest...

zigzags on the tail...

a triangular stripe...

two eyes...

and a nose.

(4)

(5)

(6)

## Try this...

To make your fox look like it's sitting down, draw the head, face and ears as above, then add...

a body like this and a bushy tail...

zigzags on the tail...

two front legs...

and one back leg.

3

# How to draw an otter

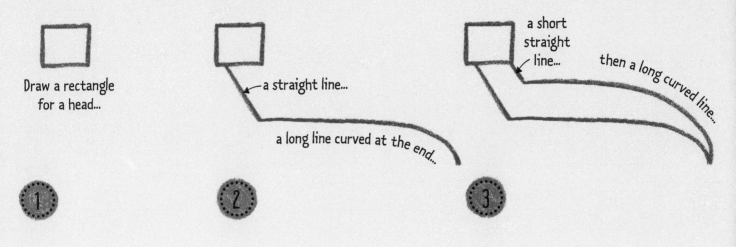

Draw a rectangle for a head...

a straight line...

a long line curved at the end...

a short straight line...

then a long curved line...

1

2

3

Your turn...

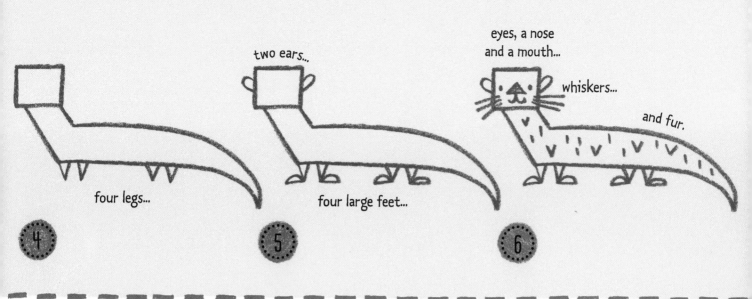

two ears...

eyes, a nose
and a mouth...

whiskers...

and fur.

four legs...

four large feet...

**4**

**5**

**6**

# How to draw a rat

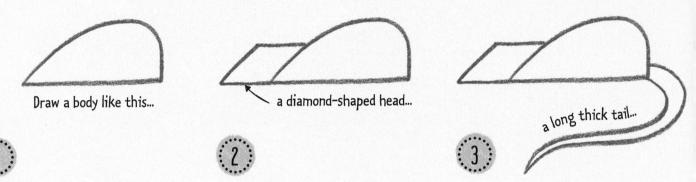

Draw a body like this...

a diamond-shaped head...

a long thick tail...

① ② ③

Your turn...

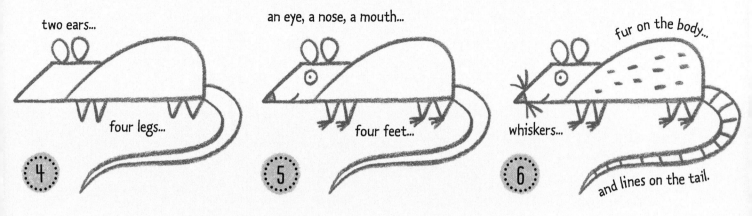

two ears...

four legs...

**4**

an eye, a nose, a mouth...

four feet...

**5**

fur on the body...

whiskers...

and lines on the tail.

**6**

## Try this...

For a sitting rat, copy the shapes below. Start with the body, then add the head and then draw the tail.

# How to draw a goat

Your turn...

1. Draw a rectangle... and a small triangle...

2. a leaf-shaped head... a tail...

3. two teardrop ears... four legs...

4. two horns... eyes, a nose and a mouth... fur... and four hooves.

# How to draw a raccoon

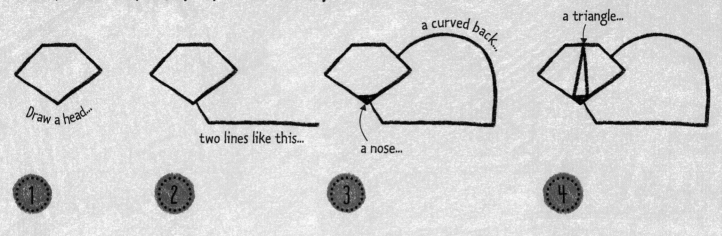

Draw a head...

two lines like this...

a curved back...

a nose...

a triangle...

1

2

3

4

Your turn...

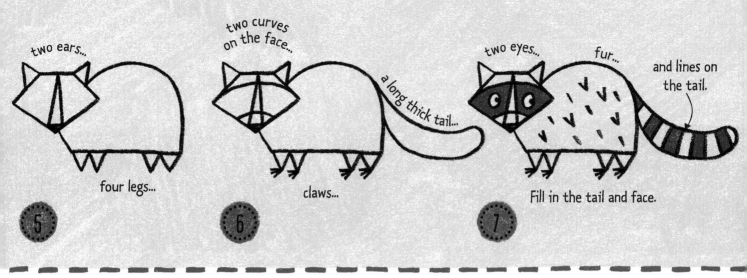

two ears...

four legs...

**5**

two curves on the face...

a long thick tail...

claws...

**6**

two eyes...

fur...

and lines on the tail.

Fill in the tail and face.

**7**

# How to draw a chipmunk

Your turn...

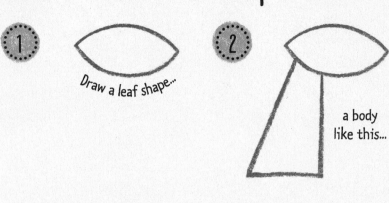

**1** Draw a leaf shape...

**2** a body like this...

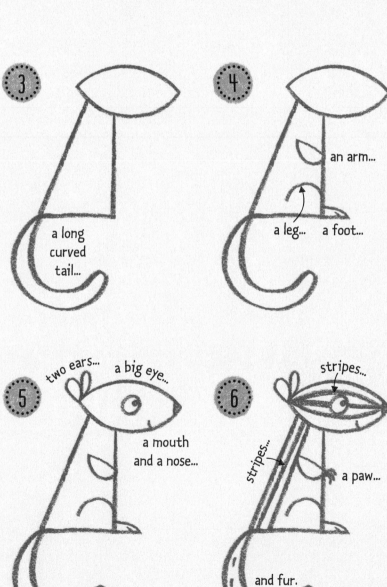

**3** a long curved tail...

**4** an arm...

a leg... a foot...

**5** two ears... a big eye...

a mouth and a nose...

**6** stripes...

stripes...

a paw...

and fur.

# How to draw a hedgehog

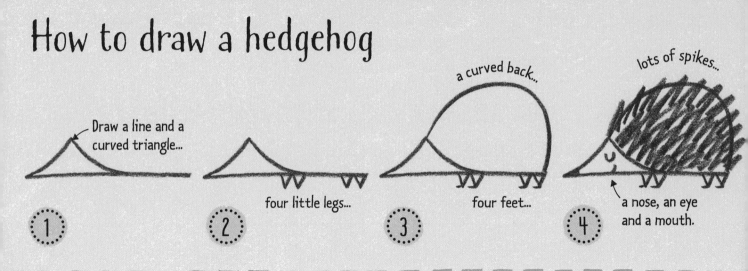

Draw a line and a curved triangle...

1

four little legs...

2

a curved back...

four feet...

3

lots of spikes...

a nose, an eye and a mouth.

4

Your turn...

# How to draw a badger

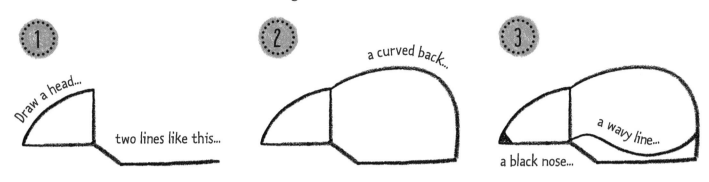

**1** Draw a head... two lines like this...

**2** a curved back...

**3** a black nose... a wavy line...

Your turn...

**4** a leaf shape... a tail...
four legs...

**5** two ears...
an eye and a mouth...
four feet...

**6** and *fur.*
Fill in the shapes like this.

# How to draw a wolf

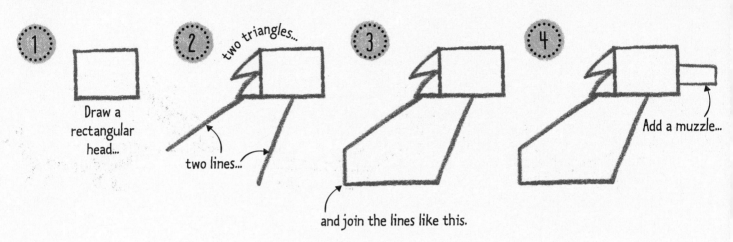

**1** Draw a rectangular head...

**2** two triangles... two lines...

**3** and join the lines like this.

**4** Add a muzzle...

Your turn...

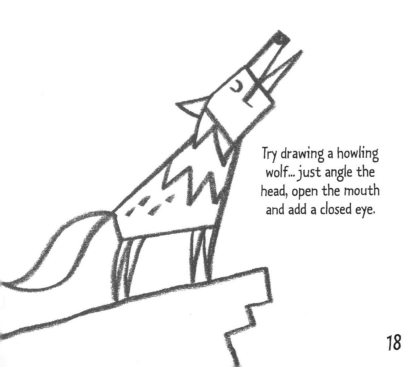

Try drawing a howling wolf... just angle the head, open the mouth and add a closed eye.

**5** four legs...

**6** two pointed ears... a bushy tail... a line for the mouth...

**7** eyes and a nose... sharp teeth... and fur.

# How to draw a grasshopper

Your turn...

1. Draw a body like this...

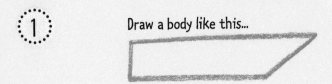

2. a leaf-shaped head...

a triangle...

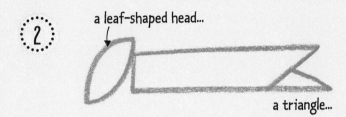

3. a line...

four legs...

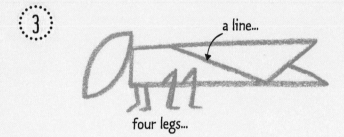

4. a large back leg...

5. feelers...

a large eye...

a mouth...

and stripes.

# How to draw a beetle

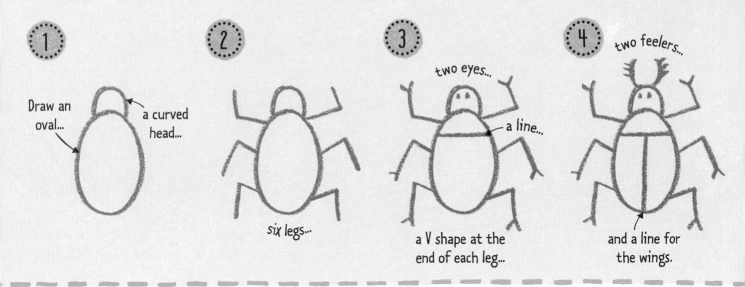

**1**

Draw an oval...

a curved head...

**2**

six legs...

**3**

two eyes...

a line...

a V shape at the end of each leg...

**4**

two feelers...

and a line for the wings.

Your turn...

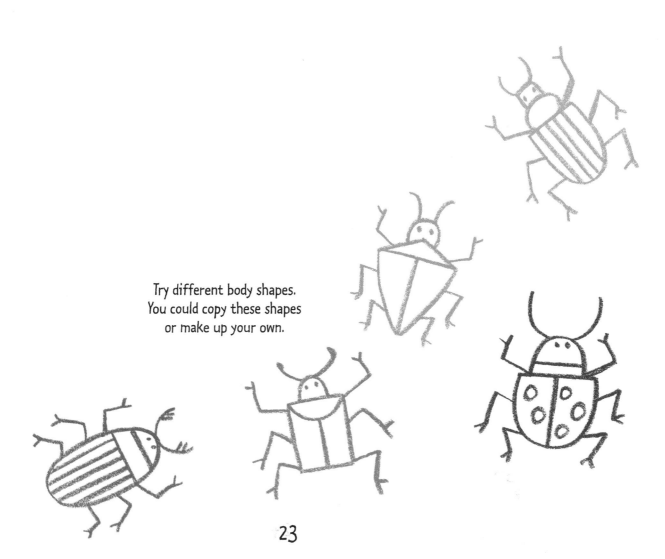

Try different body shapes.
You could copy these shapes
or make up your own.

23

# How to draw a snail

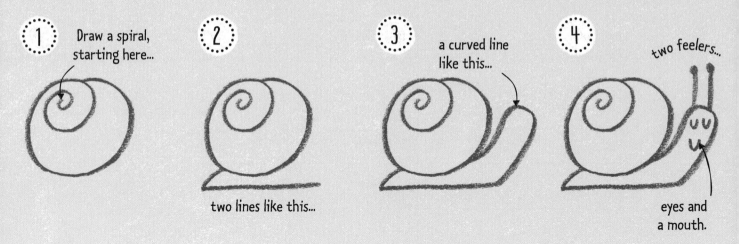

**1** Draw a spiral, starting here...

**2** two lines like this...

**3** a curved line like this...

**4** two feelers... eyes and a mouth.

Your turn...

Try this... vary the shape of the spiral and decorate to make different shells for your snail. How about...

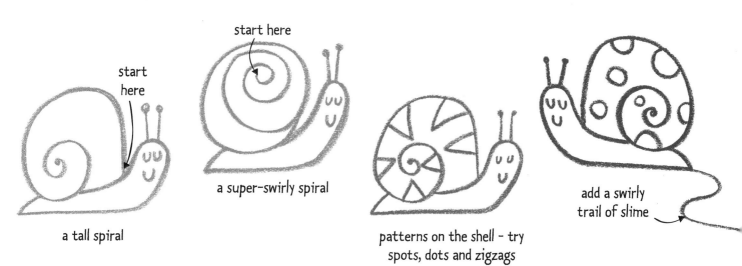

start here

start
here

a tall spiral

a super-swirly spiral

patterns on the shell - try
spots, dots and zigzags

add a swirly
trail of slime

# How to draw a butterfly

Your turn...

**1**

Draw a long petal shape...

**2**

two large wings...

**3**

a face...

two smaller wings...

**4**

two feelers...

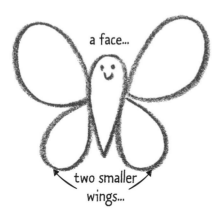

spots on the top wings...

and stripes on the body.

stripes on the bottom wings...

Try drawing some butterflies
with different patterns on
their wings.

# How to draw a jellyfish

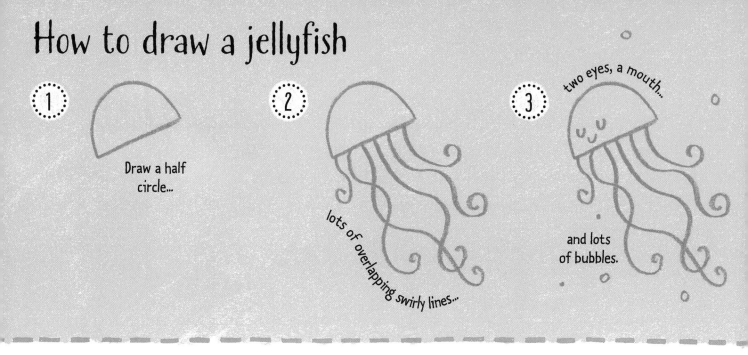

1 Draw a half circle...

2 lots of overlapping swirly lines...

3 two eyes, a mouth... and lots of bubbles.

Your turn...

# How to draw a squid

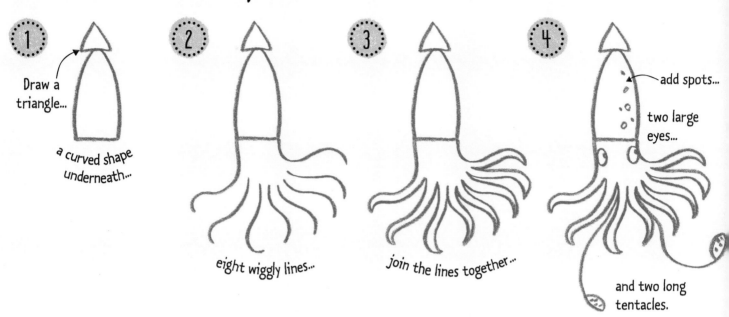

**1** Draw a triangle... a curved shape underneath...

**2** eight wiggly lines...

**3** join the lines together...

**4** add spots... two large eyes... and two long tentacles.

Your turn...

# How to draw a crab

Your turn...

1 Draw an oval...

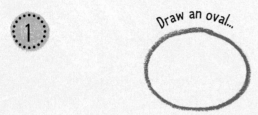

2 two lines...

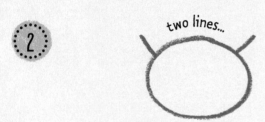

3 two large claws...

4 two lines...

four little legs on each side...

5 two eyes...

and a mouth.

Try this... change the shape of the crab's body and alter the position of the claws.

claws in different positions

a leaf-shaped body and short claws

a rectangular body and long claws

# How to draw a turtle

Your turn...

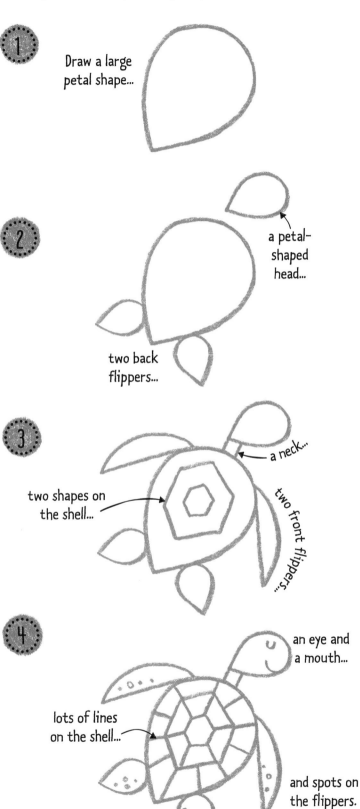

**1** Draw a large petal shape...

**2** a petal-shaped head...

two back flippers...

**3** a neck...

two shapes on the shell...

two front flippers...

**4** an eye and a mouth...

lots of lines on the shell...

and spots on the flippers.

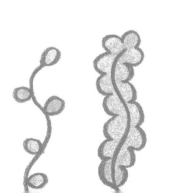
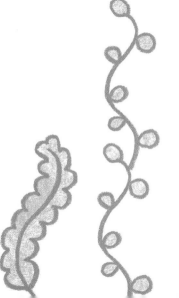

# How to draw a seahorse

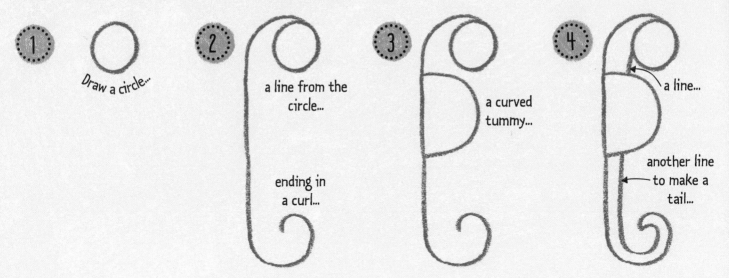

**1** Draw a circle...

**2** a line from the circle... ending in a curl...

**3** a curved tummy...

**4** a line... another line to make a tail...

Your turn...

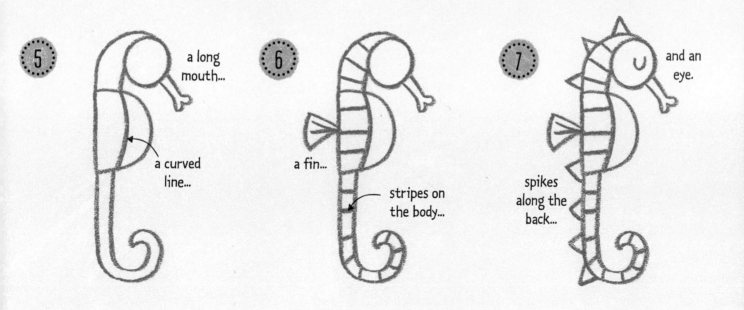

**5** a long mouth...

a curved line...

**6** a fin...

stripes on the body...

**7** and an eye.

spikes along the back...

# How to draw a parrot

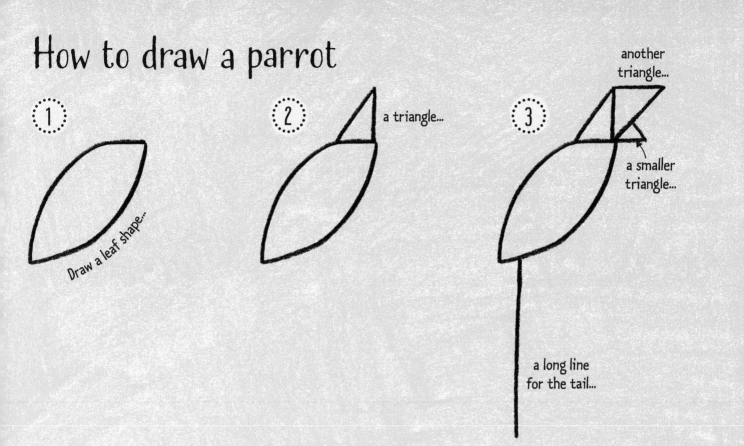

① Draw a leaf shape...

② a triangle...

③ another triangle...

a smaller triangle...

a long line for the tail...

Your turn...

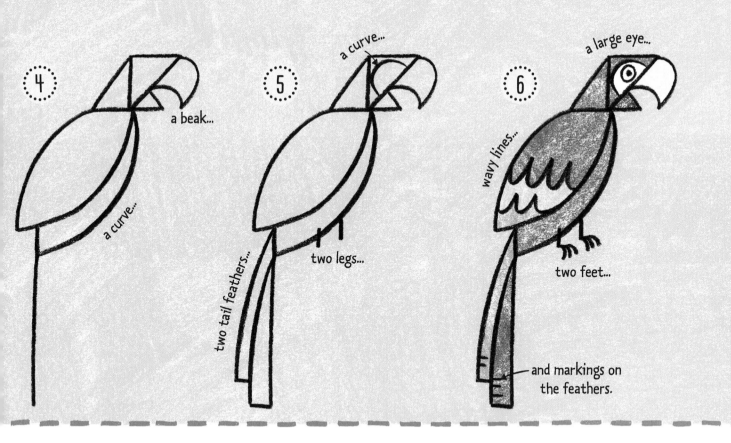

**4** a beak...

a curve...

**5** a curve...

two tail feathers...

two legs...

**6** a large eye...

wavy lines...

two feet...

and markings on
the feathers.

# How to draw a pelican

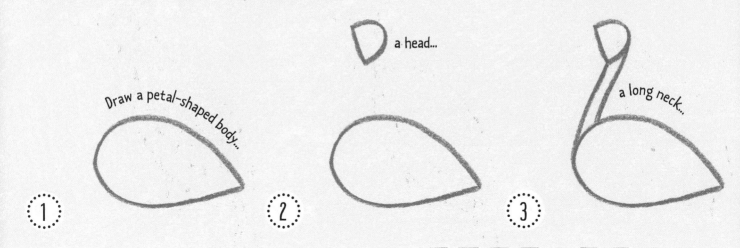

Draw a petal-shaped body...

a head...

a long neck...

① ② ③

Your turn...

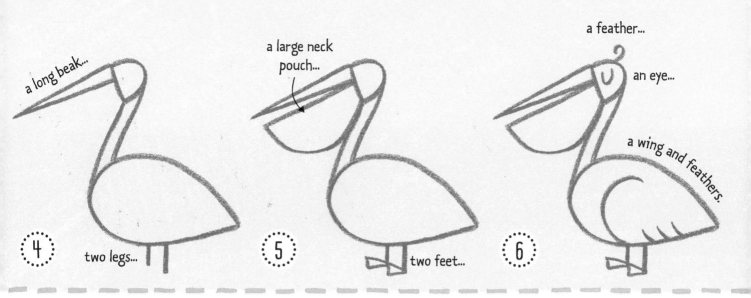

a long beak...

two legs...

④

a large neck
pouch...

two feet...

⑤

a feather...

an eye...

a wing and feathers.

⑥

# How to draw a puffin

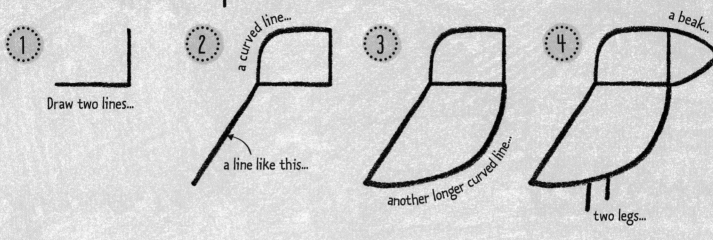

**1** Draw two lines...

**2** a curved line... a line like this...

**3** another longer curved line...

**4** a beak... two legs...

Your turn...

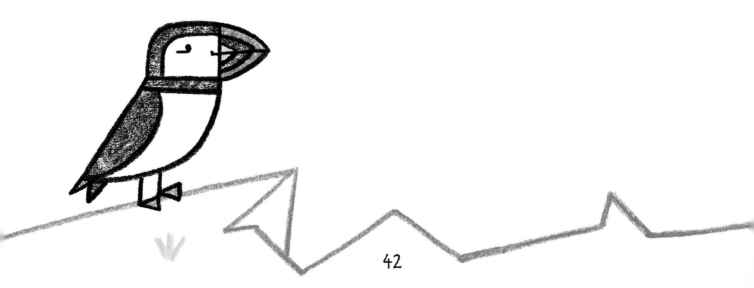

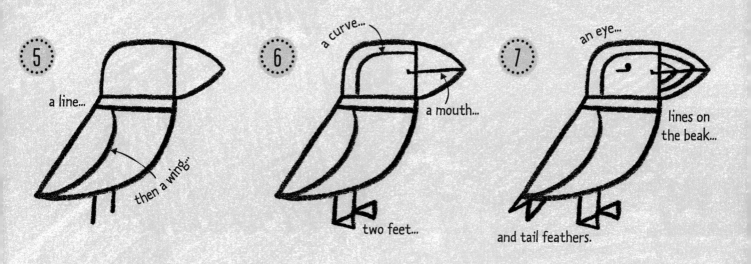

5 a line... then a wing...

6 a curve... a mouth... two feet...

7 an eye... lines on the beak... and tail feathers.

# How to draw a toucan

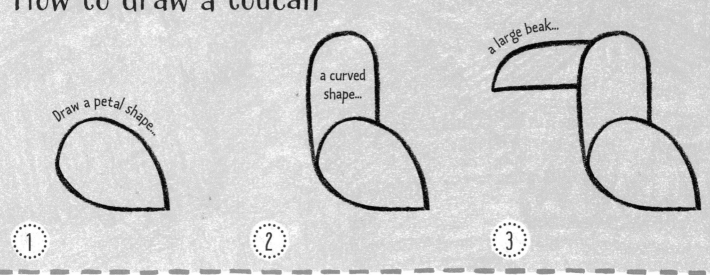

Draw a petal shape...

① 

a curved shape...

②

a large beak...

③

Your turn...

**4** a straight line... a curved line...

**5** another line... two legs... a tail...

**6** a curve... an eye... feathers... and feet.

## Try this...

Once you have drawn your toucan, you could use red, green, blue, yellow and black pens or pencils to fill it in like this.

# How to draw a vulture

**1** Draw a petal shape...

**2** a curve inside...

**3**

a rectangle...

Your turn...

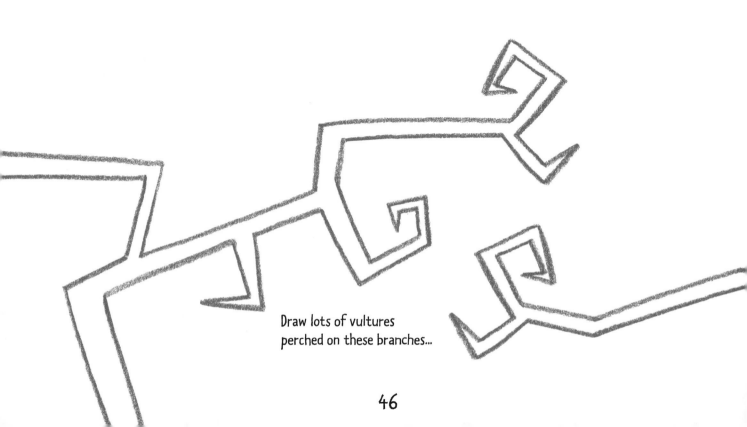

Draw lots of vultures
perched on these branches...

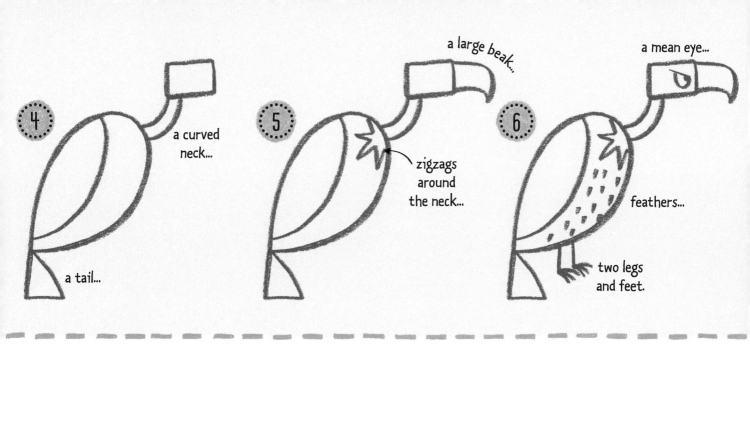

**4** a curved neck...

a tail...

**5** a large beak...

zigzags around the neck...

**6** a mean eye...

feathers...

two legs and feet.

# How to draw a hummingbird

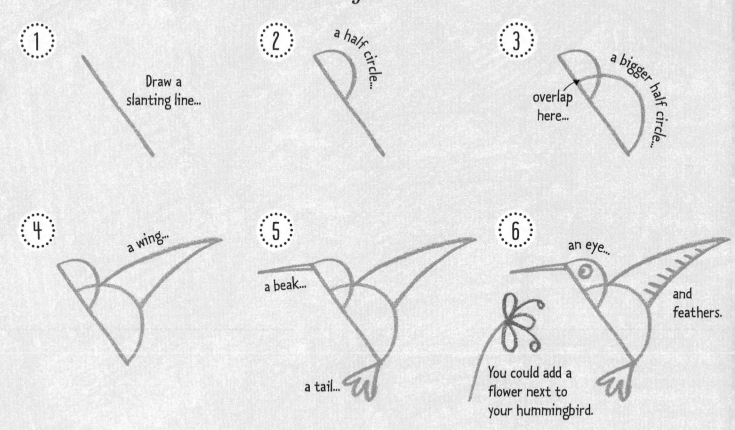

① Draw a slanting line...

② a half circle...

③ overlap here... a bigger half circle...

④ a wing...

⑤ a beak... a tail...

⑥ an eye... and feathers. You could add a flower next to your hummingbird.

Your turn...

# How to draw an anteater

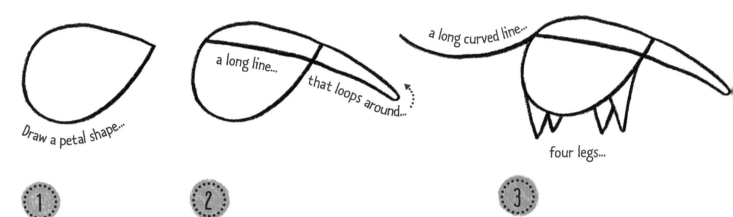

Draw a petal shape...

a long line...

that loops around...

a long curved line...

four legs...

1

2

3

Your turn...

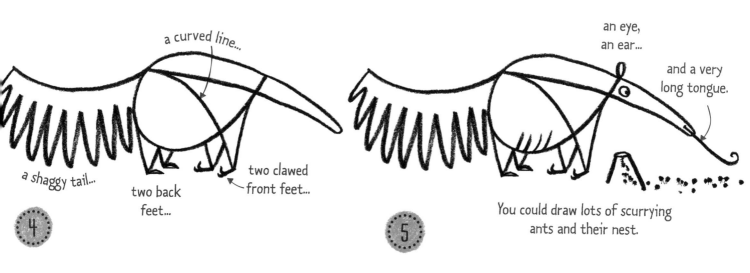

a curved line...

a shaggy tail...

two back feet...

two clawed front feet...

an eye, an ear...

and a very long tongue.

**4**

**5**

You could draw lots of scurrying ants and their nest.

# How to draw a sloth

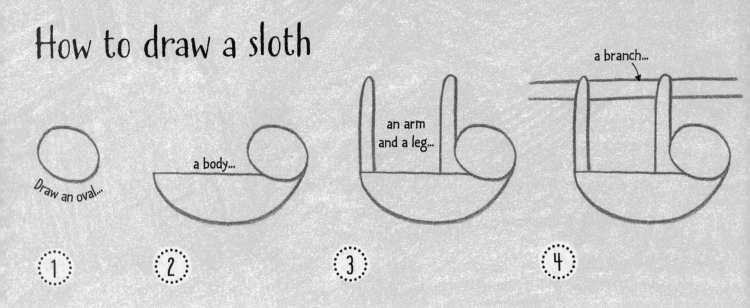

Draw an oval...

**1**

a body...

**2**

an arm and a leg...

**3**

a branch...

**4**

Your turn...

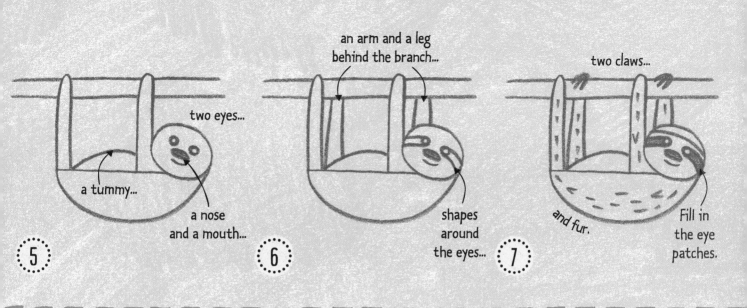

two eyes...

a tummy...

a nose
and a mouth...

5

an arm and a leg
behind the branch...

shapes
around
the eyes...

6

two claws...

and fur.

Fill in
the eye
patches.

7

# How to draw a chameleon

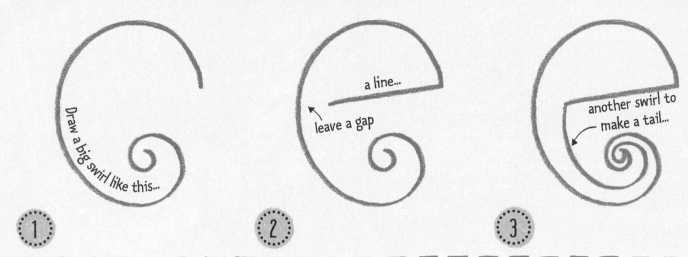

1 Draw a big swirl like this...

2 a line... leave a gap

3 another swirl to make a tail...

Your turn...

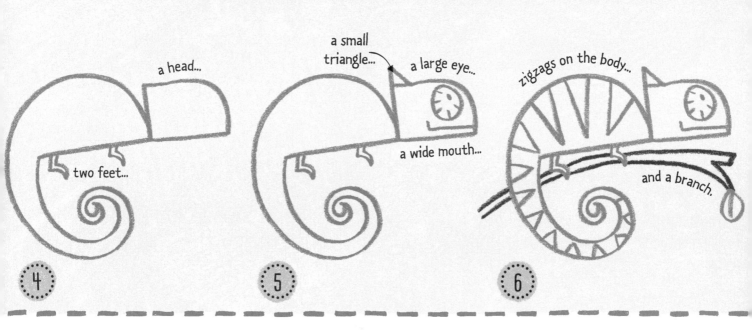

a head...

two feet...

4

a small triangle...

a large eye...

a wide mouth...

5

zigzags on the body...

and a branch.

6

55

# How to draw a hippo

Your turn...

**1**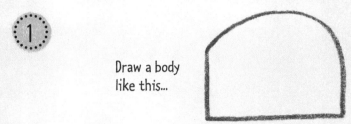

Draw a body like this...

**2**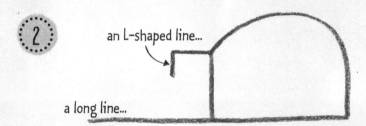

an L-shaped line...

a long line...

**3**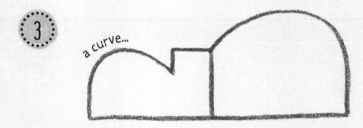

a curve...

**4**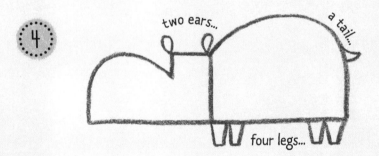

two ears...

a tail...

four legs...

**5**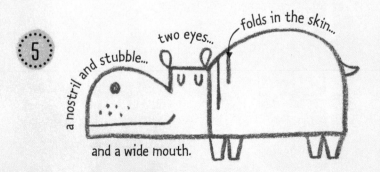

folds in the skin...

two eyes...

a nostril and stubble...

and a wide mouth.

# Try this...

For a hippo wallowing in a muddy lake, don't draw the legs. Just draw little curved lines around the hippo's body to show the ripples in the water.

# How to draw a leopard

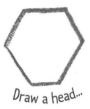

Draw a head...

**1**

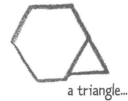

a triangle...

**2**

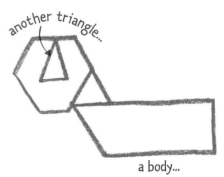

another triangle...

a body...

**3**

- - - - - - - - - - - - - - - - - - - - - - - - - - -

Your turn...

58

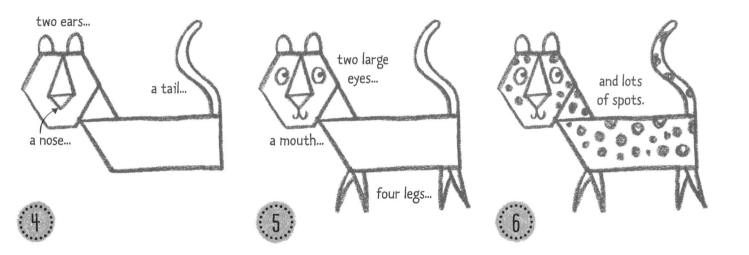

two ears...

a nose...

a tail...

**4**

two large eyes...

a mouth...

four legs...

**5**

and lots of spots.

**6**

## Try this...

To draw a leopard in a tree, follow the instructions above. When you get to step 4, don't draw the tail up in the air but hanging down. At step 5, draw the eyes and mouth, then copy the legs as shown below. Then add a branch for your leopard to lie on.

# How to draw a meerkat

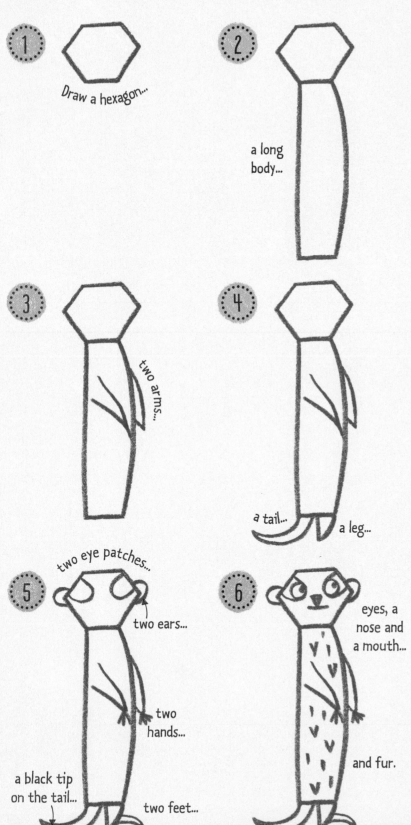

**1** Draw a hexagon...

**2** a long body...

**3** two arms...

**4** a tail... a leg...

**5** two eye patches... two ears... two hands... a black tip on the tail... two feet...

**6** eyes, a nose and a mouth... and fur.

Your turn...

# How to draw a gorilla

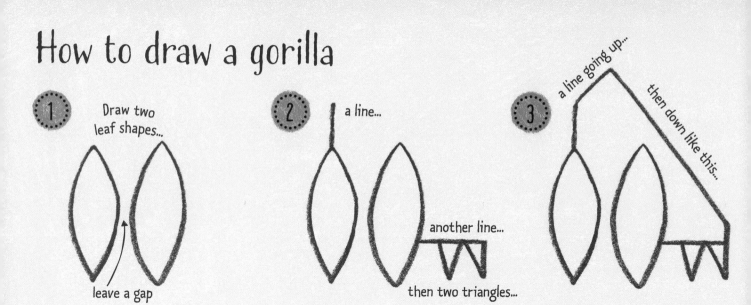

**1** Draw two leaf shapes...

leave a gap

**2** a line...

another line...

then two triangles...

**3** a line going up...

then down like this...

Your turn...

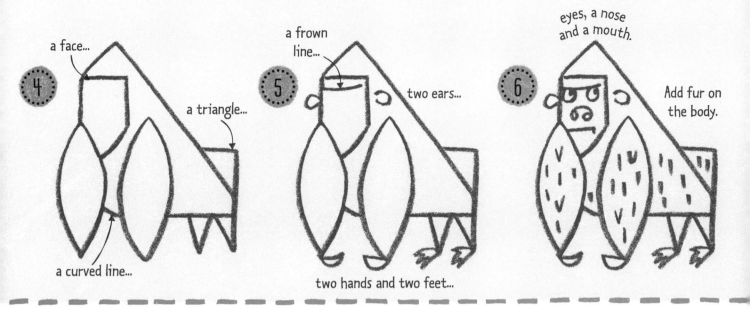

**4** a face...

a triangle...

a curved line...

**5** a frown line...

two ears...

two hands and two feet...

**6** eyes, a nose and a mouth.

Add fur on the body.

## Try this...

To make your gorilla stand out even more, instead of adding fur marks, fill it in with scribbly lines. Don't fill in the face, ears, hands and feet.

# How to draw a giraffe

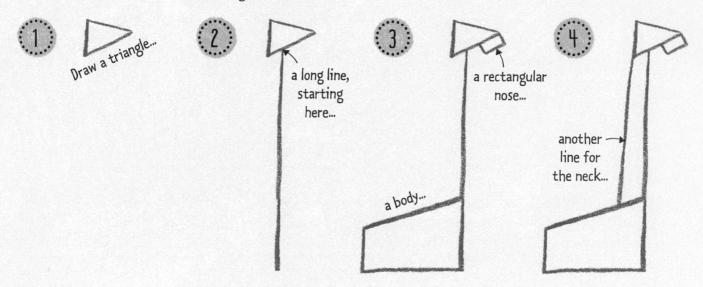

1 Draw a triangle...

2 a long line, starting here...

3 a body...

4 a rectangular nose...

another line for the neck...

Your turn...

**5** a mouth...

four long legs...

**6** two ears...

a mane along the neck...

a tail...

four wide feet...

**7** two horns...

an eye...

a nostril...

and lots of spots.

# How to draw an armadillo

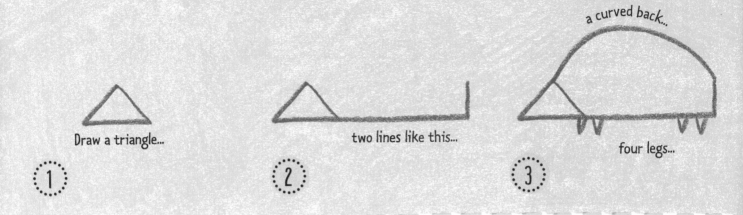

Draw a triangle...

1

two lines like this...

2

a curved back...

four legs...

3

Your turn...

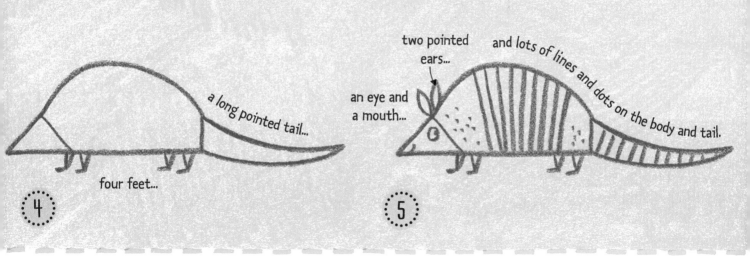

a long pointed tail...

four feet...

two pointed ears...

an eye and a mouth...

and lots of lines and dots on the body and tail.

(4)

(5)

# How to draw a bushbaby

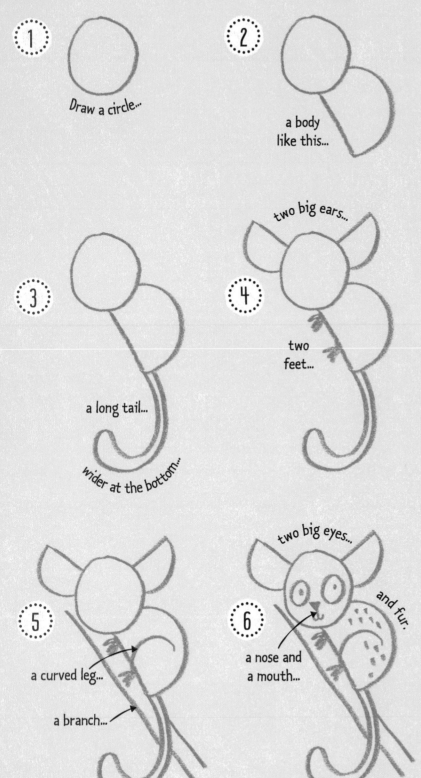

**1** Draw a circle...

**2** a body like this...

**3** a long tail... wider at the bottom...

**4** two big ears... two feet...

**5** a curved leg... a branch...

**6** two big eyes... and fur. a nose and a mouth...

Your turn...

# How to draw a zebra

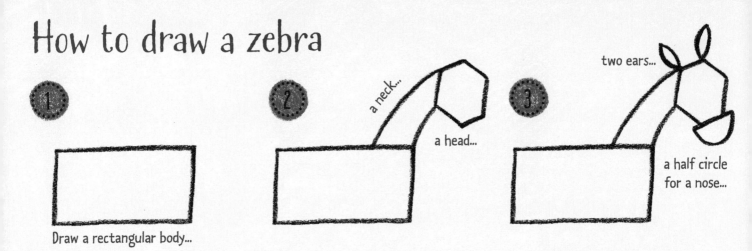

**1** Draw a rectangular body...

**2** a neck... a head...

**3** two ears... a half circle for a nose...

Your turn...

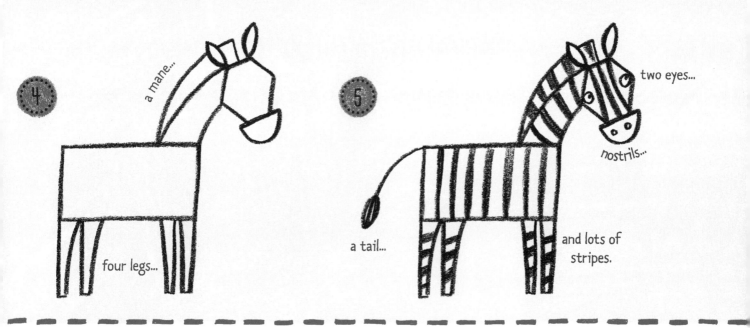

4 a mane...

four legs...

5 two eyes...

nostrils...

a tail...

and lots of stripes.

# How to draw a rhino

**1** Draw this shape for the body...

**2** a curved line... and another...

**3** the back of the head... a mouth and a snout...

**4** four legs...

**5** two ears... two horns... a tail...

**6** folds in the skin... an eye and a nostril.

Your turn...

# How to draw a scorpion

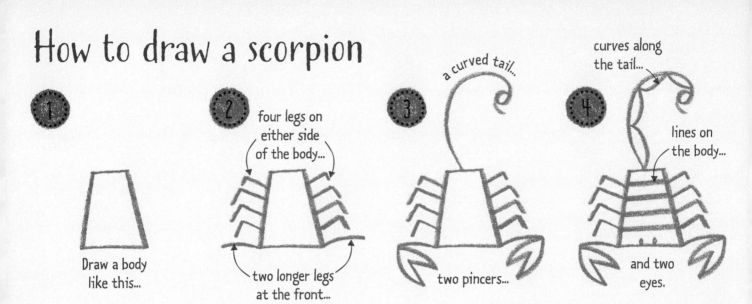

**1** Draw a body like this...

**2** four legs on either side of the body...

two longer legs at the front...

**3** a curved tail...

two pincers...

**4** curves along the tail...

lines on the body...

and two eyes.

Your turn...

# How to draw a koala

Your turn...

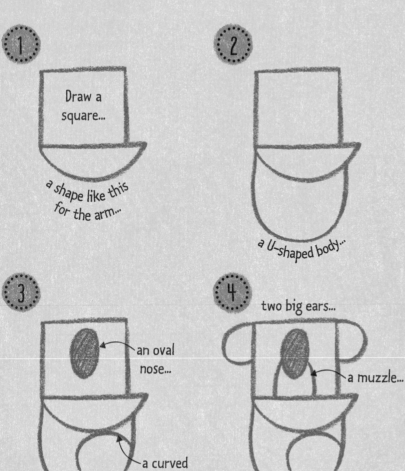

**1** Draw a square... a shape like this for the arm...

**2** a U-shaped body...

**3** an oval nose... a curved leg...

**4** two big ears... a muzzle...

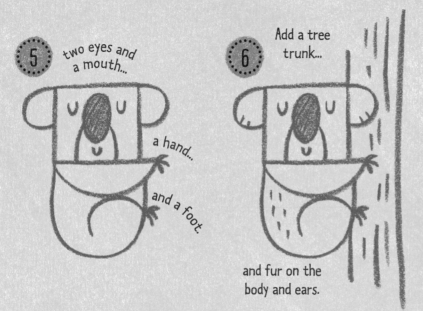

**5** two eyes and a mouth... a hand... and a foot.

**6** Add a tree trunk... and fur on the body and ears.

# How to draw a kangaroo

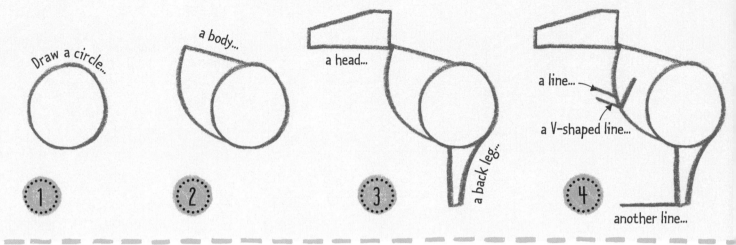

Draw a circle...

1

a body...

2

a head...

a back leg...

3

a line...

a V-shaped line...

another line...

4

Your turn...

5 a hand... a thick tail... the top of the foot...

6 two ears... an eye, a nose and a mouth... and fur.

## Try this...

Draw a jumping kangaroo by changing the position of the back leg. You could also add a baby joey in a pouch.

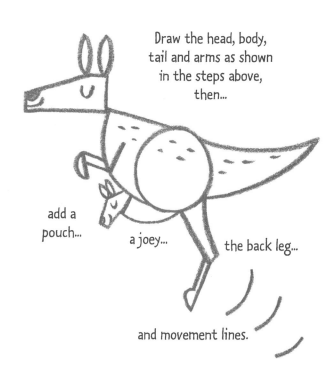

Draw the head, body, tail and arms as shown in the steps above, then...

add a pouch...

a joey...

the back leg...

and movement lines.

# How to draw a llama

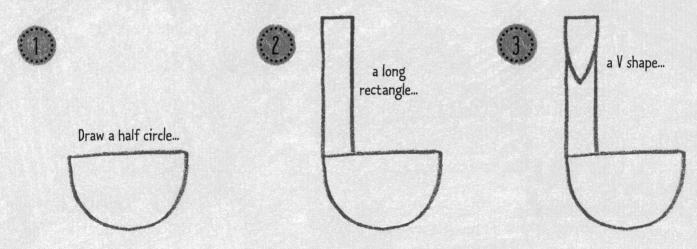

**1** Draw a half circle...

**2** a long rectangle...

**3** a V shape...

Your turn...

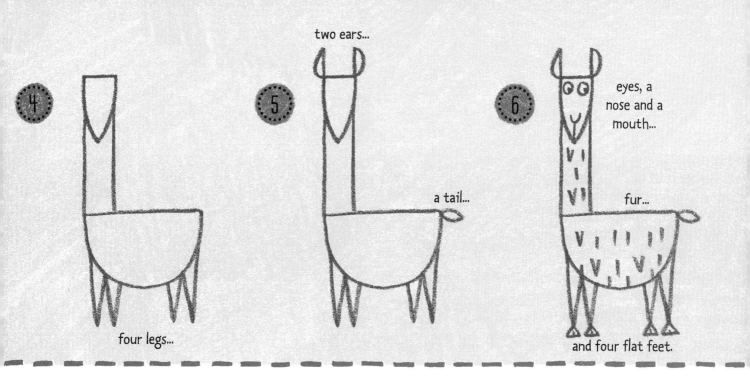

**4** four legs...

**5** two ears...
a tail...

**6** eyes, a nose and a mouth...
fur...
and four flat feet.

# How to draw a camel

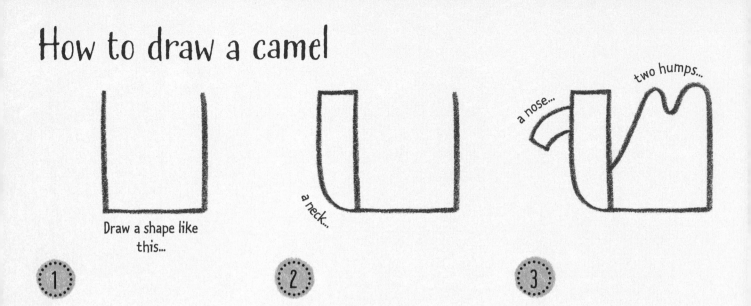

**1** Draw a shape like this...

**2** a neck...

**3** a nose... two humps...

Your turn...

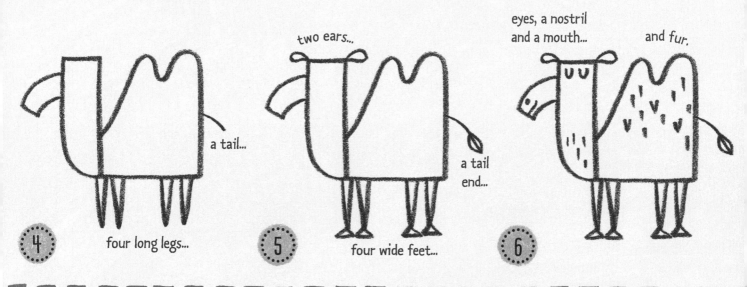

two ears...

eyes, a nostril and a mouth...

and *fur*.

a tail...

a tail end...

**4** four long legs...

**5** four wide feet...

**6**

## Try this...

Some camels have only one hump. You could try copying the shape of this camel's body.

# How to draw a polar bear

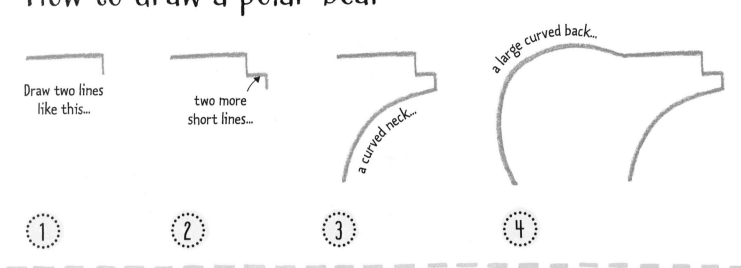

Draw two lines like this...

two more short lines...

a curved neck...

a large curved back...

① ② ③ ④

Your turn...

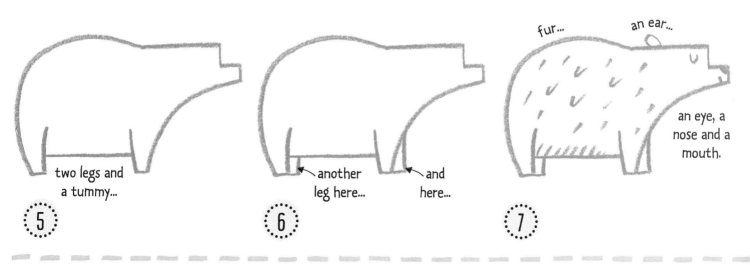

two legs and
a tummy...

**5**

another
leg here...

and
here...

**6**

fur...

an ear...

an eye, a
nose and a
mouth.

**7**

# How to draw a whale

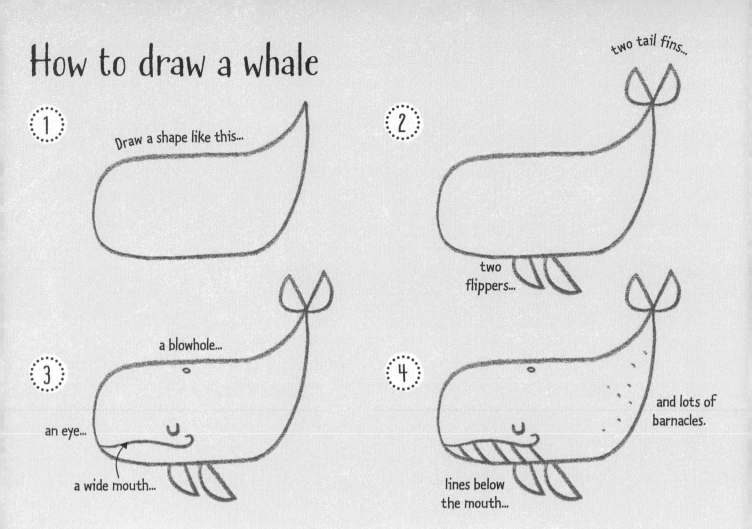

① Draw a shape like this...

② two tail fins...

two flippers...

③ a blowhole...

an eye...

a wide mouth...

④ and lots of barnacles.

lines below the mouth...

Your turn...

# How to draw a walrus

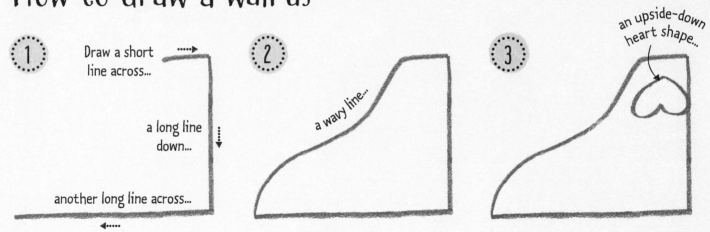

**1** Draw a short line across...

a long line down...

another long line across...

**2** a wavy line...

**3** an upside-down heart shape...

Your turn...

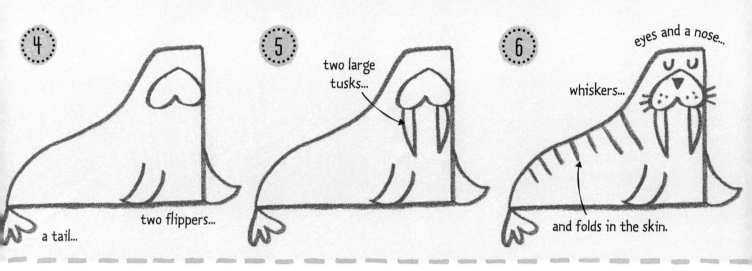

**4** a tail... two flippers...

**5** two large tusks...

**6** eyes and a nose... whiskers... and folds in the skin.

# At the zoo

The following pages have ideas for scenes created from pictures in the book. Use the ideas to finish drawing the scenes, you could then fill them in with pens or pencils.

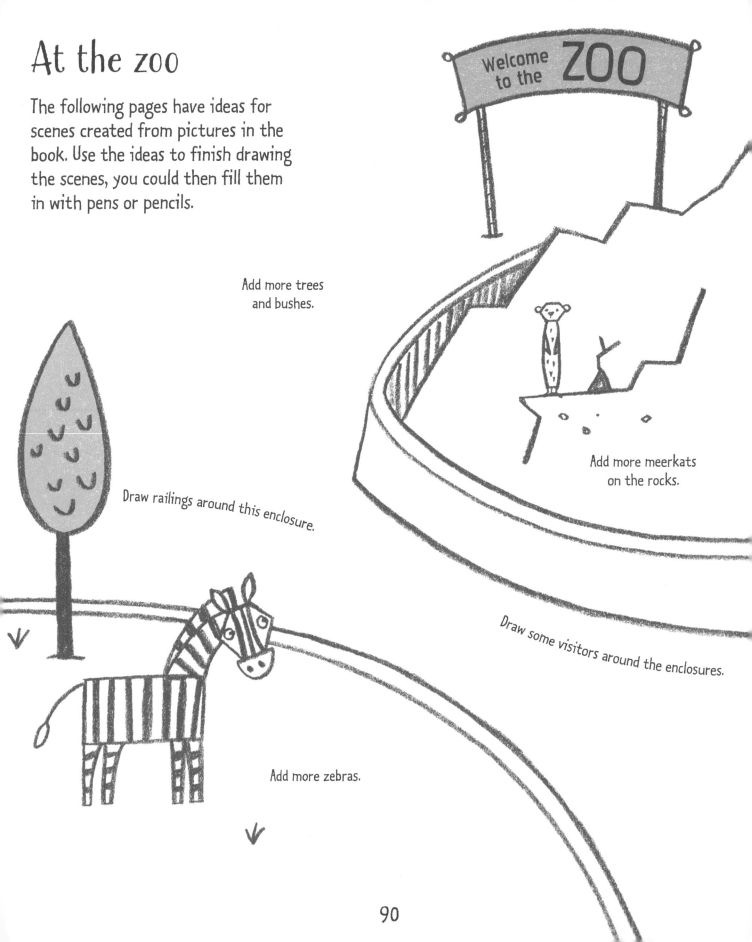

Welcome to the ZOO

Add more trees and bushes.

Draw railings around this enclosure.

Add more meerkats on the rocks.

Draw some visitors around the enclosures.

Add more zebras.

Draw a gorilla family.

Add a baby giraffe.

# In the rainforest

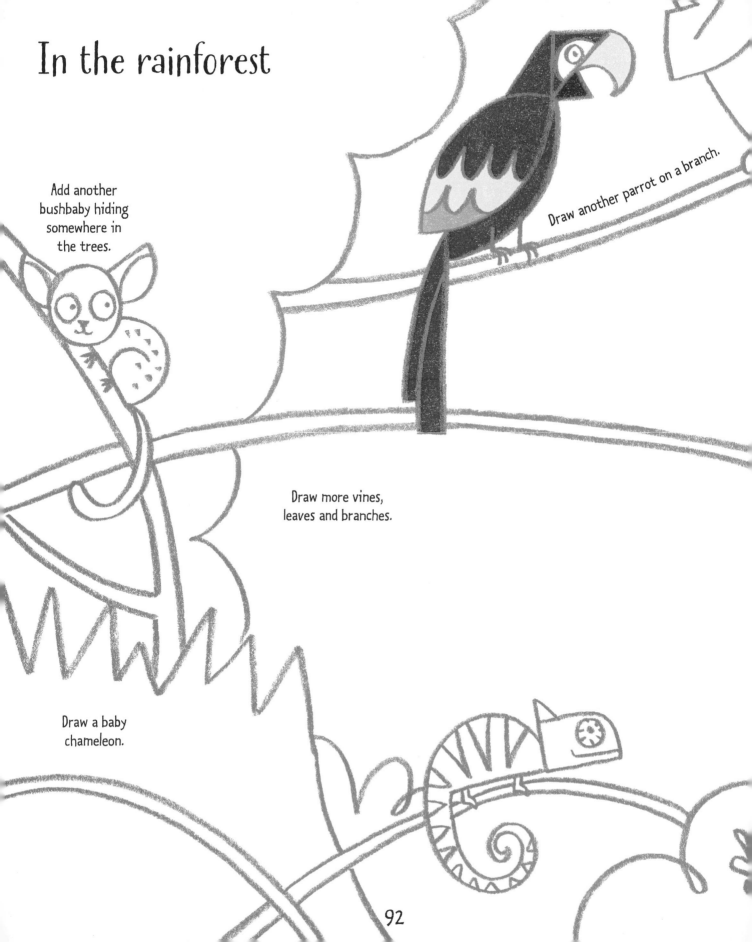

Add another bushbaby hiding somewhere in the trees.

Draw another parrot on a branch.

Draw more vines, leaves and branches.

Draw a baby chameleon.

Add another hanging sloth.

Add another toucan.

and tropical flowers.

fluttering butterflies...

Draw more hovering hummingbirds...

93

# Under the sea

Draw lots of little
fish like these,
swimming together.

Draw another
squid.

Draw more
seahorses hiding
in the coral.

Add more jellyfish.

You could copy these larger fish too.

Draw more coral...

and seaweed.

95

# Bugs

Draw butterflies in
the sky...

and beetles on leaves.

and more slimy snails.

Add another grasshopper...

First published in 2015 by Usborne Publishing Ltd., Usborne House, 83-85 Saffron Hill, London EC1N 8RT, England.
www.usborne.com © 2015 Usborne Publishing Ltd. The name Usborne and the devices 🎈 🎈 are Trade Marks of Usborne Publishing Ltd.